T0126584

THE LITTLE BOOK OF

SUNSHINE

Published in 2024 by OH!
An Imprint of Welbeck Non-Fiction Limited,
part of Welbeck Publishing Group.
Offices in: London – 20 Mortimer Street, London W1T 3JW
and Sydney – Level 17, 207 Kent St, Sydney NSW 2000 Australia
www.welbeckpublishing.com

Disclaimer:

OH! encourages diversity and different viewpoints. However, all views, thoughts, and opinions expressed in this book are not necessarily representative of Welbeck Publishing Group as an organization. All material in this book is set out in good faith for general guidance; no liability can be accepted for loss or expense incurred in following the information given. In particular, this book is not intended to replace expert medical or phychiatric advice. It is intended for informational purposes only and for your own personal use and guidance. It is not intended to diagnose, treat or act as a substitute for professional medical advice.

ISBN 978-1-80069-557-3

Compiled and written by: Victoria Denne
Design: Stephen Cary
Project manager: Russell Porter
Production: Jess Brisley

A CIP catalogue record for this book is available from the British Library

Printed in China

10 9 8 7 6 5 4 3 2 1

THE LITTLE BOOK OF
SUNSHINE

BRINGING POSITIVITY
AND LIGHT INTO YOUR LIFE

CONTENTS

INTRODUCTION – 6

8
CHAPTER
ONE

POSITIVE VIBES
ONLY

38
CHAPTER
TWO

SILVER LININGS

58
CHAPTER
THREE

BE KIND

98

CHAPTER
FOUR

IT'S THE LITTLE
THINGS

146

CHAPTER
FIVE

AFFIRMATIONS

174

CHAPTER
SIX

HERE COMES
THE SUN

INTRODUCTION

We live in a world that seems to be dominated by negativity, where uncertainty and despair are around every corner and on every news channel. It can be hard to remain positive and see the light at the end of the tunnel when we're surrounded by such doom and gloom, and yet, while there's no getting away from our problems – as individuals, as a society and as a planet – we all need a break from them every now and again.

And this is where this book comes in.

Filled to the brim with inspirational quotations and words of wisdom to help you see the brighter side to life, there are also some tried-and-tested tips and strategies to cultivate a more positive mindset. We'll also share some positive affirmations that you can use as personal mantras, ideas to bring happiness to other people's lives, as well as some of the little things that can bring untold joy to your own.

Quite simply, *The Little Book of Sunshine* is the silver lining you've been looking for. So, go on, open the window and let the light in.

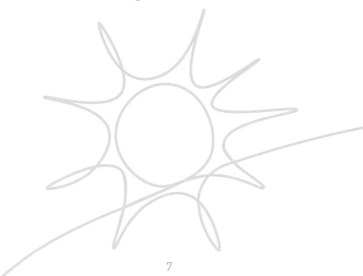

CHAPTER
1

POSITIVE
VIBES ONLY

Contrary to popular belief, *you* make the sunshine in your life. Here are some tips on how to banish clouds and stay positive...

Smile!

Smiling releases neuropeptides, which help reduce stress, as well as feel-good chemicals like dopamine, serotonin and endorphins.

What sunshine is to flowers, smiles
are to humanity. These are but
trifles, to be sure; but scattered
along life's pathway, the good they
do is inconceivable.

Joseph Addison

Laughter is a sunbeam of the soul.

Thomas Mann

Avoid negativity
by thinking positive
thoughts when
you can

There is nothing either good or bad,
but thinking makes it so.

Shakespeare, *Hamlet*

Change your thoughts and you
change your world.

Norman Vincent Peale

Pick a personal mantra
and repeat it – often!
Write it down and keep it
somewhere you
will see it every day.

See Chapter 5 for some ideas!

If you have good thoughts they will
shine out of your face like sunbeams
and you will always look lovely.

Roald Dahl, *The Twits*

Keep a
gratitude journal

Every day, try to write three
things you are grateful for. For
an extra challenge, try to make
them different every day.

Gratitude is a celebration
we are all invited to.

Cleo Wade

Meditate

Meditation has been shown to reduce stress, control anxiety, lead to improved self-image and a more positive outlook on life – among many other benefits.

Keep your face always toward
the sunshine – and shadows will
fall behind you.

Walt Whitman

Exercise

When we move our bodies, we kick up our endorphin levels, the famous "feel-good" chemicals. Even a short burst of exercise can increase our mental alertness, boost energy levels and improve mood.

Hold up your head!
You were not made for failure,
you were made for victory.

Anne Gilchrist

If we take care of the moments, the years will take care of themselves.

Maria Edgeworth

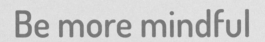

Be more mindful

Carry out tasks one at a time. Slow down. Notice the movements you make and the thoughts you are having as they come into your head.

We're so busy watching out for what's just ahead of us that we don't take time to enjoy where we are.

Bill Watterson

Act as if what you do makes
a difference. It does.

William James

**Find a hobby that makes
you really happy –
and make time for it**

It could be getting the
paintbrushes out, taking up a
sport you last played at
school – or something
completely new! The only
rule is that it brings you joy.

Write it on your heart that every
day is the best day in the year.

Ralph Waldo Emerson

Spend time
with people
who make
you feel good

Friends are the sunshine of life.

John Hay

Reduce stress by practising self-care – and don't feel guilty about it

Whether it's making that hair appointment you've been pushing back for months or taking the time to make your favourite meal – do something that renews your spirit, and make sure it's just for you.

Just living is not enough...
One must have sunshine,
freedom, and a little flower.

Hans Christian Andersen

Spend time
in nature

Nature has given us all the pieces required to achieve exceptional wellness and health, but has left it to us to put these pieces together.

Diane McLaren

O, Sunshine!
The most precious gold
to be found on earth.

Roman Payne

Live in the sunshine,
swim the sea,
drink the wild air.

Ralph Waldo Emerson

CHAPTER
2

SILVER LININGS

Not every day is filled with
sunshine, but when times
are tough, try to look for the
silver lining, even when it
seems hard to find.

Never give up. Today is hard, tomorrow will be worse, but the day after tomorrow will be sunshine.

Jack Ma

You have to do everything you can,
you have to work your hardest,
and if you do, if you stay positive,
you have a shot at a silver lining.

Pat, *Silver Linings Playbook*

When everything seems to be
going against you, remember
that the airplane takes off against
the wind, not with it.

Henry Ford

If you change the way you look at things, the things you look at change.

Wayne Dyer

There are always flowers for
those who want to see them.

Henri Matisse

The broken will always be able to love harder than most. Once you have been in the dark, you learn to appreciate everything that shines.

Zachry K. Douglas

The human capacity for burden is like bamboo – far more flexible than you'd ever believe at first glance.

Jodi Picoult

If you want to see the sunshine,
you have to weather the storm.

Frank Lane

We are the silver lining
in any and every dark cloud
we could ever find.

Tyler Knott Gregson

You never know how strong
you are until being strong is the
only choice you have.

Bob Marley

We must accept finite disappointment,
but never lose infinite hope.

Martin Luther King Jr

Believe you can and you're halfway there.

Theodore Roosevelt

I can be changed by what happens to me. But I refuse to be reduced by it.

Maya Angelou

Too many people miss the silver lining because they're expecting gold.

Maurice Setter

On the other side of a storm is
the strength that comes from
having navigated through it.
Raise your sail and begin.

Gregory S. Williams

You are loved just for being who
you are, just for existing.

Ram Dass

The same wind that blows down your house shakes berries from the bushes.

Marci Ridlon

There is always a silver lining. Find it.

Shayne Neal, *From Misery to Happiness: A Poetic Journey Through Love, Loss, and Second Chances*

CHAPTER
3

BE KIND

One of the simplest ways
to brighten your mood is to
bring a ray of sunshine to
another person's day.
Here are just a few ideas...

Pay someone
a compliment

A compliment is verbal sunshine.

Robert Orben

Tell someone what
they mean to you

A kind word is like a spring day.

Russian proverb

Remember to say thank you

Kindness and politeness are not
overrated at all. They're underused.

Tommy Lee Jones

Smile at everyone
you encounter
for a day

Today, give a stranger one of your smiles. It might be the only sunshine he sees all day.

H. Jackson Brown, Jr

Too often we underestimate
the power of a touch, a smile,
a kind word, a listening ear,
an honest compliment, or the
smallest act of caring,
all of which have the potential
to turn a life around.

Leo Buscaglia

Give up your seat on public transport to someone who might need it more than you

Sometimes it takes only one
act of kindness and caring to
change a person's life.

Jackie Chan

Introduce two
people you think
might get on

Share your umbrella
with someone who
has been caught out
by a downpour

It is the characteristic
of the magnanimous man
to ask no favour but to be ready
to do kindness to others.

Aristotle

Carry out a random act of kindness,
with no expectation of reward, safe
in the knowledge that one day
someone might do the same for you.

Princess Diana

Hold the door open
for a stranger

Send a friend
or loved one a
handwritten letter

What you do makes a difference,
and you have to decide what kind of
difference you want to make.

Jane Goodall

You can get everything in life you
want if you will just help enough other
people get what they want.

Zig Ziglar

Let someone
with just a few
items ahead
of you in the
checkout queue

Remember, there's no such thing as a small act of kindness. Every act creates a ripple with no logical end.

Scott Adams

Make a personalized playlist for a loved one

Love and kindness are never wasted.
They always make a difference.
They bless the one who receives
them, and they bless you, the giver.

Barbara De Angelis

Just finished
a great book?
Give it to a
friend to read

Start a conversation
with a stranger

Those who bring sunshine
into the lives of others cannot
keep it from themselves.

J. M. Barrie

Send new parents
a care package
of yummy treats

Spread love everywhere you go.
Let no one ever come to you
without leaving happier.

Mother Teresa

If you can,
donate blood

A kind gesture can reach a wound that only compassion can heal.

Steve Maraboli

Send a postcard to someone you've lost touch with to let them know you are thinking of them

Buy someone a
bunch of flowers,
or pick some from
your own garden

Flowers always make people better, happier, and more helpful; they are sunshine, food and medicine to the mind.

Luther Burbank

Cook a meal for
someone who's
feeling stressed

When you give joy to other people,
you get more joy in return. You should
give a good thought to happiness
that you can give out.

Eleanor Roosevelt

Volunteer at an animal shelter

Check in with
someone you sense
might be going
through a hard time.
Then just *listen*.

Always be a little kinder than necessary.

James M. Barrie

CHAPTER
4

IT'S THE LITTLE THINGS

It's often the simplest pleasures
in life that bring us the most joy, if
only we stop to appreciate them.

You don't need fancy things to feel good. You can hug a puppy. You can buy a can of paint and surround yourself with colour. You can plant a flower and watch it grow. You can decide to start over and let other people start over too.

Joan Bauer

I think it's important to find
the little things in everyday life
that make you happy.

Paula Cole

I'd rather have roses on my table
than diamonds on my neck.

Emma Goldman

Bring flowers
into your home

Take a bubble bath

Sorrow can be alleviated by good sleep,
a bath and a glass of wine.

St Thomas Aquinas

Revel in the feeling
of the cool side of
your pillow.

The little things amount to big things.

Robin S. Sharma

Anything can make me stop and look
and wonder, and sometimes learn.

Kurt Vonnegut

Carry out a random act of kindness

See Chapter 3 for ideas!

Well, your greatest joy definitely comes from doing something for another, especially when it was done with no thought of something in return.

John Wooden

A nice warm shower, a cup of tea,
and a caring ear may be all you need
to warm your heart.

Charles F. Glassman

Pop bubble wrap –
just for the fun of it!

It's the simple things in life that are the most extraordinary; only wise men are able to understand them.

Paulo Coelho

Get up early and catch a sunrise – or stay up and watch the sun set somewhere beautiful

There's a sunrise and a sunset every single day, and they're absolutely free. Don't miss so many of them.

Jo Walton

Sit on a park bench
and just *be*

For a while, I was left with nothing on the physical plane. I had no relationships, no job, no home, no socially defined identity. I spent almost two years sitting on park benches in a state of the most intense joy.

Eckhart Tolle, *The Power of Now*

She often climbed up the hill and lay there alone for the mere pleasure of feeling the wind and of rubbing her cheeks in the grass. Generally at such times she did not think of anything, but lay immersed in an inarticulate well-being.

Edith Wharton, *The Age of Innocence*

Sometimes, if you stand on the bottom rail of a bridge and lean over to watch the river slipping slowly away beneath you, you will suddenly know everything there is to be known.

A. A. Milne

When you find out who you are,
you find out what you need.

Mama Odie, *The Princess and the Frog* (2009)

What could be better than to
sit besides the fire with a book and
a glowing lamp while the wind
beats outside the windows.

Gustave Flaubert, *Madame Bovary*

I have never been drawn to luxury.
I love the simple things; coffee
shops, books, and people who try to
understand.

R. Y. S. Perez

A quiet and modest life brings more joy
than a pursuit of success bound with
constant unrest.

Albert Einstein

Treat yourself to new
school supplies, even
if you left school
a long time ago...

See the world through the eyes
of your inner child. The eyes that
sparkle in awe and amazement as
they see love, magic and mystery
in the most ordinary things.

Henna Sohail

Take pleasure in
undisturbed snow

The very fact of snow is such
an amazement.

Roger Ebert

Go outside
and appreciate
the stars

If people sat outside and looked
at the stars each night, I'll bet they'd
live a lot differently.

Bill Watterson

Take the time to really savour your food and drink

Sometimes it is the smallest
thing that saves us: the weather
growing cold, a child's smile, and
a cup of excellent coffee.

Jonathan Carroll

Feel the sand
beneath your toes

If the sight of the blue skies fills
you with joy, if a blade of grass
springing up in the fields has the
power to move you, if the simple
things of Nature have a message
that you understand, rejoice, for
your soul is alive.

Eleonora Duse

Notice the beauty of nature everywhere you go

Forget about the money for a moment. Lose yourself in the wilderness, listen to the music of the softly blowing winds, feel the rain on your bare skin, let the mountains take the burden off your shoulders.

Kiran Bisht

There is nothing quite like the
smell of rain on a grass field after
a sunny spell.

Fuad Alakbarov

I wake up in the morning and I see that flower, with the dew on its petals, and at the way it's folding out, and it makes me happy.

Dan Buettner, *Thrive: Finding Happiness the Blue Zones Way*

How can one stand in a field of red poppies and not want to live forever?

Marty Rubin

To find the universal elements enough; to find the air and the water exhilarating; to be refreshed by a morning walk or an evening saunter. To be thrilled by the stars at night; to be elated over a bird's nest or a wildflower in spring – these are some of the rewards of the simple life.

John Burroughs, *Leaf and Tendril*

Remember to stroke
your furry friends

Sometimes the best thing that
can happen to a person is to have
a puppy lick your face.

Joan Bauer

Set aside time
for a really long
conversation with
a friend

A big group of daily friends or a
white painted house with bills and
mirrors, are not a necessity to me –
but an intelligent conversation while
sharing another coffee, is.

Charlotte Eriksson

Luxuriate in the feeling of sleeping in clean sheets

Sometimes, the simple things are more fun and meaningful than all the banquets in the world.

E. A. Bucchianeri

CHAPTER
5

POSITIVE AFFIRMATIONS

Never underestimate the power of words. Here are some positive affirmations to keep close and repeat daily, if you like.

I am in the right place at the right time,
doing the right thing.

Louise Hay

I am strong

I am who I am; no more, no less.

Terry Goodkind

My thoughts and feelings matter

I am a wellspring
of creativity

Conscious breathing is my anchor.

Thích Nhât Hạnh

I am an unstoppable
force of nature

My mission in life is not merely
to survive, but to thrive.

Maya Angelou

I radiate positivity

I deserve forgiveness

Make way for the unprecedented and watch your reality rearrange yourself.

Yrsa Daley-Ward

I am powerful

The mind is everything.
What you think you become.

Buddha

I am somebody. I am me.
And I don't need anybody
to make me somebody.

Louis L'Amour

I trust my instincts

Am I good enough? Yes I am.

Michelle Obama

I deserve to be
surrounded by
people who love
and respect me

The perfect moment is this one.

Kabat-Zinn

I am following
my dreams

I am living with
abundance

I am deliberate and afraid of nothing.

Audre Lord

I am not defined by my past. I am driven by my future.

I am worthy

I'm better than I used to be. Better than I was yesterday. But hopefully not as good as I'll be tomorrow.

Marianne Williamson

I love myself
unconditionally

I can be whatever
I want to be

CHAPTER

6

HERE COMES THE SUN

Now that we're feeling all warm and fuzzy, here are some final inspirational words to keep the positive vibes going...

Every day above earth
is a good day.

Ernest Hemingway

Nothing can dim the light
that shines from within.

Maya Angelou

The chance to love and be loved
exists no matter where you are.

Oprah

Rivers know this: there is no hurry.
We shall get there some day.

A. A. Milne

Life can be much broader once you discover one simple fact: Everything around you that you call life was made up by people that were no smarter than you. And you can change it, you can influence it... Once you learn that, you'll never be the same again.

Steve Jobs

Life is like riding a bicycle. To keep your balance you must keep moving.

Albert Einstein

I choose to make the rest of
my life the best of my life.

Louise Hay

We must be willing to let go of
the life we planned so as to have
the life that is waiting for us.

Joseph Campbell

If you spend your whole life
waiting for the storm, you'll never
enjoy the sunshine.

Morris West

Your life is already a miracle of chance
waiting for you to shape its destiny.

Toni Morrison

Don't let the shadows of yesterday
spoil the sunshine of tomorrow.
Live for today.

Nandina Morris

Wherever you go, no matter
what the weather, always bring
your own sunshine.

Anthony J. D'Angelo

Courage starts with showing up
and letting ourselves be seen.

Brené Brown

A cloudy day is no match for
a sunny disposition.

William Arthur Ward

May sunshine surround you each new day. And may smiles and love never be far away.

Catherine Pulsifer

Embrace the glorious
mess that you are.

Elizabeth Gilbert

Life is short. Smile while you still have teeth...

Unknown